MY CLASS
GOES TO THE
LIBRARY

MY CLASS
GOES TO THE
LIBRARY

Vivien Griffiths

meets

Angela Verma

Photography: Chris Fairclough

Franklin Watts
London/New York/Toronto/Sydney

Every day I go to school
with my childminder.

I have got some books in my bag today.
My class is going to the library.

This is my classroom.
Everybody is busy making clowns.
We are going to take them to the library.

This is our school library.
It is quite small.
We like going to the big library
down the road.

We have to put our coats on.

It is very cold and snowy outside
and it is a long way to walk.

I walk with Sumandeep.

We like to look at the shops
on the way.
This shop sells fruit and vegetables.
They are all different colours and shapes.

The road is full of noisy cars.
I press the button at the crossing.

We cross when we see the green man.

Here we are at the library.
It's a very old building, like our school.

First of all, we give our books in
at the counter.

Then we show Geeta our clowns.
She is very pleased with them.
She says she will hang them up.

We have a look at all the books.
There are books about dinosaurs,
space rockets and pets.
There are storybooks and picture books too.

Geeta always reads us stories.
We sit on the carpet in the story corner.

Geeta holds up the book
so we can all see the pictures.

Then we play a game.
Today we play The Farmer's in his Den.

Geeta is the bone.
She bends down and we all pat her,
but not too hard.

Before we go, we choose some new books
to take home.
Geeta helps us.

I always take a long time
choosing my books.

I am having a look
at the books about different countries.

Geeta stamps the date in our books.
Then we know when to bring them back.

Our tickets are kept in special trays
behind the counter until we come again.

It's time to go now.
Geeta waves us goodbye.

We all hurry back to school.

When I go home,
I take my new books in my bag.

My little brother wants a book
of his own.
I will help to choose one for him
when we go to the library on Saturday.

© 1985 Franklin Watts Limited
12A Golden Square
London W1R 4BA

ISBN 0 86313 321 5

Editor: Ruth Thomson
Design: Edward Kinsey

Printed in Belgium

The Publishers, author and photographer would like to thank the staff and pupils of Tiverton Junior and Infants School, Selly Oak, Birmingham. Thanks are also due to the staff of Selly Oak Library, especially to Geeta Pattanaik.

Vivien Griffiths is Head of Services to Children and Young People, Birmingham Public Libraries.